FRESHMAN YEAR UNLOCKED

THE ULTIMATE COLLEGE PLAYBOOK

Title: Freshman Year Unlocked:
The Ultimate College Playbook
Author: M.D. Jenkins

Copyright © 2025 Montsho Publishers. All rights reserved.

No part of this book may be reproduced, stored in a retrieval system, or transmitted in any form or by any means—electronic, mechanical, photocopying, recording, or otherwise—without the prior written permission of the author or publisher, except in the case of brief quotations embodied in critical articles or reviews.

This book is for educational and informational purposes only. The author and publisher assume no responsibility for errors, omissions, or outcomes resulting from the use of this material. Readers should consult relevant professionals when making personal, academic, or financial decisions.

First Edition
Published by Montsho Publishers, Charlotte, NC

ISBN: 978-0-9679795-8-8
Cover Design: Montsho Publishers
Printed in the United States of America

For inquiries or permissions, please contact:
customersupport@montshopublishers.com

Dedication

To every college freshman stepping into a new chapter of life—
This book is for you.

May it guide you, inspire you, and remind you that you're capable of more than you know. Here's to the late-night study sessions, the friendships you'll cherish forever, and the endless opportunities waiting for you.

You've got this.

With gratitude and encouragement,
M.D. Jenkins

M.D. JENKINS

TABLE OF CONTENTS

FIRST SEMESTER – LAYING THE FOUNDATION

BUCKET LIST	I
INTRODUCTION	01
WEEKS 1-4: SETTLING IN & BUILDING ROUTINES	08
WEEKS 5-8: ACADEMIC SUCCESS	16
WEEKS 9-16: BUILDING MOMENTUM	26

SECOND SEMESTER – GROWTH & LONG-TERM PLANNING

INTRODUCTION	43
WEEKS 1-4: STARTING FRESH	46
WEEKS 5-8: STRENGTHENING YOUR FOUNDATION	54
WEEKS 9-16: PLANNING FOR THE FUTURE	64
CONCLUSION	87
BONUS PAGES	91

Bucket List for the Year

📚 Academic & Campus Life

✅ Visit the library for something other than studying
✅ Attend office hours (even if you don't need help)
✅ Study in every major study spot on campus
✅ Get a perfect score on at least one exam or paper
✅ Form a study group before midterms
✅ Try out a class or lecture outside your major
✅ Do homework outside on a nice day
✅ Pull an (almost) all-nighter and survive the next day
✅ Sit in the front row of a big lecture just for fun
✅ Get involved in a campus research project

🎉 Social & Fun

✅ Go to a themed party or campus festival
✅ Get dressed up and attend a formal event
✅ Go to a karaoke night with friends
✅ Have a spontaneous adventure with your roommate
✅ Host a game night or movie marathon in your dorm
✅ Try an escape room with a group of friends
✅ Have a random conversation with a stranger
✅ Play a pickup game of basketball, soccer, or frisbee
✅ Take a photo in front of every campus landmark
✅ Find a fun weekend trip or getaway with friends

Bucket List for the Year

🍕 Food & Dining Challenges

- ✅ Try every item at the campus coffee shop
- ✅ Eat at least one weird food combo from the dining hall
- ✅ Find the best late-night food spot near campus
- ✅ Learn to cook a full meal in your dorm
- ✅ Host a DIY dorm dinner night with friends
- ✅ Find a restaurant with the best college student discounts
- ✅ Go one week without eating fast food (challenge yourself!)
- ✅ Try a new international cuisine you've never had before
- ✅ Order room service or delivery in the middle of the night

💰 Budgeting & Career Growth

- ✅ Open a high-yield savings account and start saving
- ✅ Apply for at least one scholarship
- ✅ Create a LinkedIn profile (or update it)
- ✅ Attend a career fair and talk to employers
- ✅ Get a resume review at the career center
- ✅ Land your first paid internship or campus job
- ✅ Practice mock interviews with a career coach or friend
- ✅ Start a side hustle to make extra money
- ✅ Make a budget and stick to it for at least a month

Bucket List for the Year

🏋️ Health & Wellness

✅ Walk 10,000+ steps in one day around campus
✅ Try a new workout class (yoga, spin, kickboxing, etc.)
✅ Meditate for 5 minutes a day for a full week
✅ Go a full day without social media
✅ Journal your thoughts for an entire week
✅ Have a self-care day with zero school stress
✅ Drink only water for a full week (goodbye soda & coffee!)
✅ Get at least 7 hours of sleep every night for a week

🛏️ Dorm Life & Campus Living

✅ Rearrange your dorm room at least once
✅ Do laundry without ruining anything
✅ Leave a random positive note for a dorm neighbor
✅ Pull a prank on your roommate or floor mates
✅ Host a themed dorm party or get-together
✅ Have a sleepover in a friend's dorm just for fun
✅ Go an entire day without using your phone in your dorm
✅ Find a hidden lounge or cool spot in your dorm building

Bucket List for the Year

🌎 Exploration & Adventure

✅ Visit every building on campus at least once
✅ Take a day trip to a nearby city or nature spot
✅ Go to a random campus event that you wouldn't normally attend
✅ Find the best scenic view on campus
✅ Take a picture with your school mascot
✅ Go on a midnight adventure around campus
✅ Explore a new coffee shop, bookstore, or park near school

🔥 The Ultimate Challenge

✅ Do something completely outside your comfort zone
✅ Find one unforgettable moment that defines your freshman year

🔥 Add Your Own Items

✅

✅

✅

✅

✅

✅

First Semester

Introduction: Welcome to the Best Year of Your Life!

Congratulations, you're officially a college freshman! This is the start of an incredible journey filled with new adventures, lifelong friendships, and opportunities to learn and grow. College is an exciting chapter of your life where you get to explore who you are, dream big, and create the foundation for your future. It's your time to shine!

But let's be honest—starting college can also feel a little overwhelming. Between juggling classes, meeting new people, managing your schedule, and figuring out where the cafeteria is (we've all been there), it's easy to feel like you're spinning plates. That's where this book comes in.

What Is This Book?

Think of this guide as your personal college cheerleader, mentor, and planner all rolled into one. This isn't just a boring manual filled with lectures about "studying hard" and "getting good grades." Nope, this is a week-by-week roadmap to help you thrive in your first year of college. Each week, you'll find actionable tips, motivational advice, and fun challenges designed to help you crush your freshman year—academically, socially, and personally.

Why Is It Week-by-Week?

Life in college moves fast. One minute you're unpacking boxes in your dorm, and the next, you're cramming for finals. By breaking the year into weekly chunks, this guide helps you tackle everything one step at a time. No stress. No overwhelm. Just small, manageable actions that add up to BIG RESULTS.

Each week is like a building block—designed to help you:

- Build confidence and navigate your new environment.
- Learn how to study smarter (not harder).
- Balance school, social life, and self-care.
- Plan your future while enjoying the present.

By the end of the year, you'll not only survive college—you'll thrive, with skills, habits, and memories that will carry you through the rest of your college experience and beyond.

How to Use This Book

Here's how you can make the most out of this guide:

1. **Follow Along Each Week:** Read the section for the current week and focus on the tips and challenges. They're designed to match what you're likely experiencing at that point in the semester.
2. **Take Notes:** Use the margins or a separate notebook to jot down your thoughts, reflections, or "aha!" moments as you go.
3. **Check Off the Action Steps:** At the end of each week, there's a quick checklist of actions to take. Crossing these off will feel SO satisfying, trust me!
4. **Make It Your Own:** Everyone's college experience is unique. Use this guide as a framework, but adapt it to fit your goals, personality, and schedule.

What This Book Will Help You Do

- Make friends and build a community on campus.
- Stay on top of your classes without losing sleep or sanity.
- Manage your money like a pro (goodbye, broke college student stereotype!).
- Prepare for exams, internships, and future opportunities.
- Have fun and enjoy the heck out of your freshman year.

You've Got This!

Remember, no one has it all figured out on Day 1, and that's okay. College is all about learning, both inside and outside the classroom. You'll make mistakes, try new things, and grow in ways you never imagined. And with this guide by your side, you'll have the tools and confidence to navigate it all like a champ.

So, grab your favorite highlighter, a cozy spot to sit, and let's dive in! Together, we'll make this the best year of your life. Ready? Let's go!

✉️ Dear Future Me...

(A Letter to My Future Self)

Take a moment to reflect on where you are right now—your goals, your dreams, your worries, and your excitement for the future. Write a letter to your future self that you'll open at the end of your freshman year. What do you hope to accomplish? What advice do you want to give yourself? What are you most excited about?

📅 Date: _____

_____

_____

_____

_____

_____

_____

_____

_____

✉ Dear Future Me...

✉ Dear Future Me…

✍️ **My Hopes & Goals for Freshman Year:**
-
-
-

📌 **What I'm Excited (or Nervous) About Right Now:**
-
-
-

📌 **One Piece of Advice I Want to Remember:**
-

📜 **How to Use This Letter:**

- **Write honestly!** You'll be surprised at how much can change in a year.
- **Seal it away** (or store it digitally) and set a reminder to read it at the end of the year.
- **Compare your growth**—celebrate your wins, laugh at your worries, and reflect on your journey.

🚀 **Future You, Keep Pushing Forward! You Got This!**

Week 1: Welcome to Campus Life!

Actionable Tips

- **Explore your campus.** Find your classrooms, library, dining hall, gym, and key administrative offices like financial aid and student services. Familiarize yourself with the layout of campus to avoid feeling lost later.
- **Attend all orientation activities.** These sessions might feel repetitive, but they're crucial for meeting people, learning campus resources, and getting insider tips from upperclassmen.
- **Set up your tech.** Make sure your student email, learning portal, and Wi-Fi are working. Download apps like your school's mobile app or a digital planner to stay organized.
- **Create a basic schedule.** Plan out your class times, meals, study blocks, and downtime. Keeping some structure will help you stay on top of everything from day one.
- **Introduce yourself.** Say hello to your roommates, suite-mates, or neighbors in your dorm. Everyone's in the same boat, so breaking the ice early makes it easier to connect.

Motivational Advice

"Congratulations—you've made it! This is your chance to create the life you've always dreamed of. Sure, the first week can be overwhelming, but remember that everyone around you is feeling the same way. Take it one step at a time and trust that you belong here. Don't let small nerves hold you back from big opportunities—this is YOUR time to shine!"

Fun Challenges

- **Say hi to five strangers.** It could be someone in your dorm, a classmate, or someone you meet in the dining hall. Bonus points if you learn their names and what they're studying!
- **Try something new.** Attend a club fair or campus event, even if it's outside your comfort zone. Sign up for one activity that interests you.
- **Explore your surroundings.** Take a walk or bike ride around the area outside of campus. Find a coffee shop, park, or hidden gem nearby to make it feel like home.

Weekly Checklist

- Attend all orientation activities.
- Set up your student email and learning portal.
- Plan a basic weekly schedule.
- Meet your roommate(s) and neighbors.
- Explore the campus and locate key buildings.
- Say hello to five new people.
- Attend at least one campus event or club fair.

📌 **Tip:** Take a photo of your class schedule and save it as your phone's lock screen. This makes it easy to check where you need to be without pulling out a paper copy or searching for it online.

Week 2: Finding Your Flow

Actionable Tips

- **Finalize your schedule.** Now that classes have started, adjust your weekly schedule to include time for studying, meals, exercise, and downtime.
- **Attend every class.** Even if it's a large lecture, showing up is key to building good habits and getting familiar with your professors' teaching styles.
- **Start taking notes.** Develop a note-taking system that works for you, such as Cornell notes, outlines, or digital notes. Review your notes after each class to reinforce learning.
- **Organize your materials.** Create separate folders (physical or digital) for each class. Keep your syllabi handy and note major deadlines on your calendar.
- **Explore campus resources.** Visit the library, tutoring center, or writing lab to see what's available. Knowing where to go when you need help can save time and stress later.

Motivational Advice

"Building routines takes time, but this week is all about finding what works for you. Remember: It's not about being perfect; it's about staying consistent. Showing up, staying organized, and taking small steps every day will help you thrive. You've got this!"

Fun Challenges

- **Introduce yourself to your professors.** Stop by their office hours, even if it's just to say hello and introduce yourself. This small effort can go a long way in building connections.
- **Join a club or organization.** If you found something interesting at last week's club fair, attend a meeting or event. It's a great way to meet like-minded people.
- **Explore the dining hall.** Try something new this week—whether it's a type of food you've never had or a meal station you usually avoid. College is the perfect time to expand your palate.

Weekly Checklist

- Attend all classes and arrive on time.
- Organize your folders and syllabi for each class.
- Write down all major assignments and deadlines in your planner.
- Introduce yourself to at least one professor during office hours.
- Visit one campus resource, such as the library or tutoring center.
- Attend at least one club meeting or event.
- Try something new at the dining hall.

📌 **Tip:** Start a "master to-do list" for the semester. Use a planner or app to write down all major deadlines, exams, and assignments from your syllabi, so nothing sneaks up on you.

Week 3: Building Connections and Confidence

Actionable Tips

- **Connect with classmates.** Sit next to someone new in each class and strike up a conversation. Exchange contact information with a few classmates in case you need to collaborate or share notes.
- **Join or form a study group.** Organize a group for your trickiest class, or join an existing one. Studying with others can help you grasp concepts faster and build friendships.
- **Create a weekly review habit.** Dedicate an hour or two at the end of the week to review your notes, check your progress on assignments, and plan for the upcoming week.
- **Learn campus shortcuts.** Take time to explore your campus and discover faster ways to get to class, quieter study spots, or hidden hangout areas.
- **Start small with participation.** If you're nervous about speaking up in class, aim to ask one question or make one comment this week. It's a great way to build confidence.

Motivational Advice

"By now, you're starting to find your rhythm—and it's the perfect time to build deeper connections and lean into your strengths. Remember, college isn't just about academics; it's about growing as a person. Step out of your comfort zone a little this week—you might surprise yourself with how much you can accomplish!"

Fun Challenges

- **Plan a mini-adventure.** Grab a new friend and explore a part of campus or your college town you haven't visited yet. **Bonus:** Find a cool café, park, or local attraction to make it memorable.
- **Attend a campus event.** Look for something fun, like a sports game, concert, or cultural event. These are great opportunities to meet people and take a break from studying.
- **Learn one new skill.** Whether it's how to do laundry (yes, it counts!) or something fun like basic cooking, pick a small skill to add to your repertoire this week.

Weekly Checklist

- Sit next to a new classmate and introduce yourself.
- Exchange contact information with at least two classmates.
- Join or form a study group for one class.
- Review your notes and assignments for the week.
- Explore campus to find a new study or relaxation spot.
- Participate in at least one class by asking a question or making a comment.
- Attend a campus event or plan a fun outing with friends.

📌 **Tip:** Make it a goal to learn one new person's name every day this week. Repeating their name when you meet them helps you remember and makes a great impression.

Week 4: Finding Balance and Staying Healthy

Actionable Tips

- **Prioritize self-care.** College life can be busy, but taking care of yourself is essential. Make time for proper meals, hydration, exercise, and at least 7-8 hours of sleep each night.
- **Set boundaries.** Learn to say "no" to commitments that feel overwhelming. Balancing academics, social life, and personal time is key to avoiding burnout.
- **Stick to a budget.** Review your spending so far and adjust if needed. Track expenses using a budgeting app or a simple notebook to stay in control of your finances.
- **Check in with yourself.** Reflect on how the first few weeks have gone. Are you staying on top of your studies? Are there habits you want to improve? Make small adjustments as needed.
- **Discover campus wellness resources.** Whether it's counseling, fitness classes, or meditation groups, explore options that can help you maintain your physical and mental health.

Motivational Advice

"Remember, you can't pour from an empty cup. Taking care of yourself isn't selfish—it's necessary. College is a marathon, not a sprint, so pace yourself and prioritize your well-being. When you feel good, you perform better in every area of life. You're doing amazing—keep going!"

Fun Challenges

- **Try a new workout.** Whether it's a yoga class, a quick run around campus, or a YouTube workout in your dorm, find a way to get moving and boost your energy.
- **Plan a self-care day.** Take one evening this week to relax and recharge. Watch a movie, take a bubble bath, or read for fun—whatever helps you unwind.
- **Cook or prepare a meal.** If you have access to a kitchen, try making a simple meal or snack. If not, experiment with putting together a creative dining hall combo.

Weekly Checklist

- Get at least 7-8 hours of sleep each night.
- Stay hydrated by drinking water throughout the day.
- Stick to your budget and track your expenses.
- Reflect on your first month—what's working and what can you improve?
- Visit at least one wellness resource on campus (counseling, gym, etc.).
- Try a new workout or attend a fitness class.
- Take one evening for a personal self-care day.

📌 **Tip:** Pack healthy snacks like granola bars, nuts, or fruit in your bag. This keeps you fueled between classes and helps you avoid vending machine temptations.

Keep it up

Week 5: Study Smarter, Not Harder

Actionable Tips

- **Find your best study method.** Experiment with techniques like the Pomodoro method, mind mapping, or Cornell notes to discover what works for you. Stick with the one that helps you retain the most information.
- **Schedule dedicated study time.** Block out specific times for studying and stick to them. Treat it like an appointment you can't miss.
- **Eliminate distractions.** Create a study environment free from distractions. Use apps like Forest or Focus@Will to stay on task, or study in a quiet space like the library.
- **Review and summarize weekly.** Spend time at the end of the week summarizing what you've learned in each class. This will make midterms and finals prep much easier.
- **Use campus resources.** Visit tutoring centers, attend professor office hours, or join supplemental instruction groups to strengthen your understanding of challenging topics.

Motivational Advice

"Your success isn't just about how much time you spend studying—it's about how effectively you use that time. Focus on working smarter and creating systems that make learning feel less overwhelming. You're capable of more than you realize, so don't be afraid to push yourself a little further this week!"

Fun Challenges

- **Find your study zone.** Explore different places on campus to find where you feel most focused—whether it's the library, a quiet coffee shop, or even outside under a tree.
- **Create a "study playlist."** Put together a playlist of music that helps you focus and motivates you to stay productive. **Bonus:** Share it with a friend.
- **Reward yourself.** Plan a small treat for yourself after each productive study session. It could be a snack, a quick break to scroll your phone, or an episode of your favorite show.

Weekly Checklist

- Experiment with at least one new study technique.
- Block out time on your calendar for daily study sessions.
- Review and summarize notes from all your classes this week.
- Visit one campus resource for academic support (e.g., tutoring, office hours).
- Find and commit to a distraction-free study spot.
- Create a playlist or set up an environment that motivates you to study.
- Treat yourself after completing a focused study session.

📌 **Tip:** Dedicate one notebook or digital folder for tracking concepts or questions you don't understand during class. Use this to guide your study sessions or office hour visits.

Week 6: Midterm Prep and Staying Ahead

Actionable Tips

- **Plan your study schedule for midterms.** Review your syllabus and mark all your midterm dates and deadlines on your calendar. Break down your study material into manageable chunks for each subject.
- **Prioritize difficult subjects.** Focus more time on classes or topics you're struggling with. Start with the toughest material when your energy is at its peak.
- **Use active study techniques.** Don't just read your notes—quiz yourself, create flashcards, and practice solving problems or writing essays.
- **Attend review sessions and office hours.** Many professors or TAs will offer review sessions before midterms—take advantage of them to clarify concepts and ask questions.
- **Get organized.** Create a checklist for each class, including topics to review, practice exams to complete, and questions to clarify.

Motivational Advice

"Midterms may feel overwhelming, but this is your chance to show yourself what you're capable of. Preparation is your secret weapon! Take it one step at a time, stay consistent, and remind yourself that you're not just working for grades—you're building a foundation for success. You've got this!"

Fun Challenges

- **Plan a study group.** Team up with classmates to review material and share insights. Plus, it makes studying more fun and less lonely.
- **Create a visual study tool.** Draw a mind map, make a colorful chart, or use sticky notes to organize key concepts. **Bonus:** Hang it where you'll see it often!
- **Treat yourself after exams.** Plan a post-midterm celebration, like a movie night, a special meal, or a fun outing with friends. It'll keep you motivated to finish strong.

Weekly Checklist

- Write down all midterm dates and deadlines in your calendar.
- Create a study plan that breaks material into daily chunks.
- Focus extra time on challenging subjects or topics.
- Use active study techniques like flashcards or self-quizzing.
- Attend a professor's office hours or a midterm review session.
- Organize your notes and materials for easy access.
- Plan a fun activity or treat to reward yourself after midterms.

📌 **Tip:** Color-code your notes or study guides by subject or topic. The visual organization can help you quickly find and focus on key material during study sessions.

Week 7: Managing Stress and Staying Motivated

Actionable Tips

- **Practice stress management techniques.** Try deep breathing, meditation, or yoga to help calm your mind. Even a 10-minute break can make a big difference.
- **Stick to your routines.** Keep up with your class schedule, study sessions, and self-care habits. Routines provide stability during busy times.
- **Break tasks into smaller steps.** If you're feeling overwhelmed, focus on completing one small task at a time. Celebrate progress, no matter how small.
- **Take care of your body.** Eat balanced meals, drink water, and get enough sleep. Your mind works best when your body feels good.
- **Ask for help if you need it.** Reach out to professors, TAs, or campus resources if you're struggling with academics or personal challenges. Support is always available.

Motivational Advice

"Stress is normal—it means you care about what you're doing. But remember, you're not alone, and you're stronger than you think. Take things one day at a time, trust your abilities, and don't forget to celebrate how far you've come. You're doing great, even if it doesn't feel like it in the moment!"

stay positive

Fun Challenges

- **Schedule a mini "me day."** Block out an hour or two to do something that makes you happy—watch a movie, listen to music, or go for a walk.
- **Write down three wins from this week.** They can be big (acing a quiz) or small (waking up on time every day). Reflecting on your successes helps keep you motivated.
- **Try a creative outlet.** Whether it's drawing, journaling, or making a playlist, find a creative way to unwind and express yourself.

Weekly Checklist

- Try at least one stress management technique, like meditation or yoga.
- Stick to your routine for classes, studying, and self-care.
- Break down a large task into smaller, manageable steps.
- Eat balanced meals, drink water, and get 7-8 hours of sleep each night.
- Reach out to someone (professor, TA, friend) for support if needed.
- Reflect on three wins from this week.
- Take at least one hour for a fun or relaxing activity.

📌 **Tip:** Start each day by writing down one positive affirmation or goal for the day. This small habit can boost your mood and keep you focused.

Week 8: Reflecting and Recharging

Actionable Tips

- **Reflect on your progress.** Take some time to evaluate how the first half of the semester has gone. Ask yourself: What's working well? What could be improved? Write down your thoughts.
- **Adjust your goals.** If you set goals at the beginning of the semester, revisit them. Are they still realistic? If not, tweak them to better fit your current situation.
- **Plan for the rest of the semester.** Look ahead at upcoming deadlines, projects, and exams. Start organizing your time to avoid last-minute stress.
- **Take a day to recharge.** Dedicate one day this week to relaxing and doing something you love. It could be sleeping in, binge-watching your favorite show, or spending time with friends.
- **Organize your space.** Clean and declutter your desk, backpack, or dorm room. A tidy space can help clear your mind and improve focus.

Motivational Advice

"You've made it halfway through the semester—take a moment to celebrate that! Reflecting on your journey so far can help you appreciate your growth and prepare for what's ahead. You're doing amazing, and now's the perfect time to recharge so you can finish strong!"

Fun Challenges

- **Write a letter to your future self.** Talk about what you've accomplished so far, your current mindset, and what you hope to achieve by the end of the semester. Seal it and open it during finals week.
- **Do something new.** Try a campus activity, visit a nearby attraction, or explore a part of campus you haven't seen before.
- **Plan a fun outing.** Organize something with your friends—go out for ice cream, see a movie, or attend a campus event to unwind and bond.

Weekly Checklist

- Reflect on your progress so far and adjust your goals.
- Create a plan for the rest of the semester, including key deadlines.
- Dedicate one day to completely relax and recharge.
- Clean and organize your desk, dorm, or workspace.
- Write a letter to your future self to read during finals week.
- Try something new or attend a campus event.
- Spend time with friends or plan a fun outing.

📌 **Tip:** Create a "highlight reel" of your first two months. Write down your favorite moments or achievements, no matter how small, to remind yourself of the progress you've made. You can use the next page.

2 Month - Highlight Reel

Use both pages to paste pictures or to write down your favorite moments or achievements, no matter how small, to remind yourself of the progress you've made.

2 Month - Highlight Reel

Week 9: Career Exploration and Building Your Future

Actionable Tips

- **Visit your career center.** Schedule an appointment to explore career options, internships, or part-time job opportunities. Learn how to access resources like resume workshops and career fairs.
- **Start your resume.** Even if you don't have much experience, include high school activities, volunteer work, and any leadership roles. Keep it simple and professional.
- **Research career interests.** Think about what excites you and start exploring potential career paths. Look for job descriptions or talk to upperclassmen in similar fields.
- **Set up a LinkedIn profile.** Begin building your professional network by connecting with classmates, professors, and mentors.
- **Attend a career event.** If your school has a career fair or workshop this week, show up and practice networking.

Motivational Advice

"It's never too early to start thinking about your future. Even small steps now—like creating a resume or exploring your interests—can set you up for big opportunities later. You don't need to have everything figured out yet, but taking action now builds momentum. Your future self will thank you!"

Fun Challenges

- **Design your dream job.** Write down what your ideal career looks like. What would you do every day? Where would you work? Let yourself dream big!
- **Research an inspiring professional.** Find someone in your field of interest and learn about their journey. What can you take away from their story?
- **Practice introducing yourself.** Create a short "elevator pitch" about who you are, what you're studying, and what excites you. Try it out on a friend or mentor.

Weekly Checklist

- Visit your career center to explore resources and opportunities.
- Start or update your resume.
- Research careers or industries that interest you.
- Set up a LinkedIn profile and connect with classmates and professors.
- Attend a career-related event (e.g., career fair or workshop).
- Write down your dream job and reflect on what excites you about it.
- Practice your elevator pitch with a friend or mentor.

📌 **Tip:** Ask an upperclassman about their internship or job experiences. Hearing their stories can give you valuable insight into career options and application tips.

Week 10: Money Management and Financial Savvy

Actionable Tips

- **Create a budget.** Track your income (allowance, part-time job, etc.) and expenses (food, books, entertainment). Use a budgeting app or a simple spreadsheet to see where your money is going.
- **Set a financial goal.** Decide on a short-term goal, like saving $50 for a fun outing or putting money aside for next semester's textbooks.
- **Avoid unnecessary spending.** Identify where you might be overspending, like eating out or online shopping, and set limits to stick to your budget.
- **Learn the basics of credit.** If you have a credit card, use it responsibly and pay it off in full each month to build good credit habits. If you don't, start researching how credit works for the future.
- **Use student discounts.** Explore student deals on software, entertainment, restaurants, and even public transportation to save money.

Motivational Advice

"Learning to manage your money now is one of the best skills you'll take into adulthood. Budgeting doesn't mean you can't enjoy yourself—it means you're in control of your choices. Start small, stay consistent, and celebrate every financial win!"

Fun Challenges

- **Have a no-spend day.** Pick one day this week where you don't spend any money at all—get creative with free activities and meals.
- **Cook a meal with friends.** Instead of eating out, plan a simple meal with your friends. It's cheaper and way more fun!
- **Find a hidden deal.** Hunt for a student discount or a free campus resource you didn't know about, like free printing or event tickets.

Weekly Checklist

- Track your income and expenses for the week.
- Create a basic budget and set a financial goal.
- Cut back on unnecessary spending and focus on essentials.
- Research or learn about building good credit habits.
- Use at least one student discount or free resource this week.
- Have a no-spend day to challenge your creativity.
- Cook a meal at home with friends instead of eating out.

📌 **Tip:** Start a "fun fund" for small rewards. Put aside a few dollars each week for guilt-free spending on treats, outings, or activities you enjoy.

Week 11: Preparing for Finals and Staying Organized

Actionable Tips

- **Review your syllabus.** Check the deadlines and requirements for all your classes. Make a list of upcoming exams, final projects, and papers.
- **Create a finals prep schedule.** Divide your study material into smaller sections and assign specific days to review each topic. Start with the most challenging subjects.
- **Organize your notes.** Gather all class notes, handouts, and resources into one place. Use folders, binders, or digital tools to keep everything accessible.
- **Use study aids.** Flashcards, practice exams, and study guides can help you focus on key concepts. Don't forget to ask professors if they offer review sessions.
- **Eliminate procrastination.** Set timers for focused study sessions and take short breaks in between. Apps like Pomodoro timers can keep you on track.

Motivational Advice

"Finals might seem intimidating, but preparation is your superpower. Remember, you've been building knowledge all semester—now it's time to show what you've learned! Stay calm, take it one subject at a time, and trust that consistent effort will pay off. You've got this!"

Fun Challenges

- **Create a study playlist.** Compile your favorite focus music to make studying more enjoyable. Share it with a friend for extra motivation.
- **Reward your progress.** Set small rewards for completing study sessions, like a treat, a walk, or an episode of your favorite show.
- **Find a new study spot.** Explore your campus to discover a fresh and inspiring place to study, like a quiet garden, a cozy corner of the library, or a new coffee shop.

Weekly Checklist

- Write down all upcoming finals, projects, and deadlines.
- Create a finals prep schedule with daily study goals.
- Organize your notes and materials for each class.
- Attend any review sessions or ask professors for clarification.
- Use study aids like flashcards or practice exams.
- Set small rewards for completing study sessions.
- Try studying in a new location to keep things fresh.

📌 **Tip:** Use flashcards to review key terms or concepts while walking to class, waiting for the bus, or standing in line. Every little bit of review adds up.

Week 12: Wrapping Up Projects and Building Momentum

Actionable Tips

- **Tackle final projects.** If you have essays, presentations, or group projects due soon, focus on making steady progress each day. Break tasks into smaller, manageable steps.
- **Review your progress.** Go through your finals prep schedule from last week and adjust as needed. Prioritize areas where you feel less confident.
- **Stay consistent.** Stick to your routines for studying, attending classes, and self-care. Consistency will help you avoid burnout and finish the semester strong.
- **Double-check deadlines.** Confirm the due dates for projects and papers to ensure nothing slips through the cracks.
- **Start early.** If you have in-class finals or presentations next week, begin preparing now to avoid last-minute stress.

Motivational Advice

"You're almost there—just a few more weeks to go! This is your chance to show yourself how much you've grown this semester. Remember, every step you take now is one less thing to worry about later. Keep the momentum going—you're closer to the finish line than you think!"

Fun Challenges

- **Create a study snack station.** Stock up on healthy (and maybe a few fun) snacks to fuel your study sessions. Bonus points if you share it with friends!
- **Schedule a mini celebration.** Plan a short outing, like coffee with friends or a quick campus event, as a reward for finishing a major project or paper.
- **Send a thank-you note.** Write a quick note or email to a professor or TA who has been especially helpful this semester. Gratitude can boost your mood and theirs!

Weekly Checklist

- Break down final projects into smaller tasks and work on them daily.
- Review and adjust your finals prep schedule if needed.
- Double-check all deadlines for projects, papers, and assignments.
- Stay consistent with your study and self-care routines.
- Start preparing for in-class finals or presentations.
- Set up a study snack station for productive sessions.
- Plan a mini celebration for completing a big task.

📌 **Tip:** Set a timer for focused work sessions, like 25 minutes of uninterrupted studying, followed by a 5-minute break. This can boost productivity and prevent burnout.

Week 13: Finals Prep and Stress Management

Actionable Tips

- **Focus on key concepts.** Review study guides, past quizzes, and your professor's lecture highlights to identify the most important material for finals.
- **Set daily goals.** Break down your study sessions into manageable chunks and set small goals for each day. For example, review two chapters or complete practice problems for one subject.
- **Use active recall.** Quiz yourself, practice problems, or teach concepts to a friend. These methods help reinforce what you've learned and reveal areas needing more focus.
- **Stick to your sleep schedule.** Avoid pulling all-nighters; your brain needs rest to retain information. Aim for 7-8 hours of sleep each night.
- **Limit distractions.** Study in a quiet environment and use apps or tools to block social media and other interruptions during study sessions.

Motivational Advice

"Finals can feel overwhelming, but you've been preparing for this moment all semester. Trust the effort you've put in and take it one step at a time. Remember: your worth isn't defined by a test score. Do your best, take care of yourself, and know that you're capable of great things!"

Fun Challenges

- **Create a motivation board.** Write or draw your goals, inspirational quotes, and what you're excited about after finals. Hang it where you can see it for extra motivation.
- **Organize a group study session.** Studying with classmates can help you tackle tough topics and make studying more fun.
- **Plan a post-finals treat.** Decide on a reward for yourself, like a fun day out, a special meal, or a relaxing self-care day, to look forward to after exams.

Weekly Checklist

- Focus on reviewing the most important concepts for each class.
- Set daily study goals and track your progress.
- Use active recall methods like quizzing yourself or teaching someone else.
- Maintain your sleep schedule (no all-nighters!).
- Study in a distraction-free environment and use tools to stay focused.
- Create a motivation board to inspire you throughout the week.
- Plan a post-finals reward as something to look forward to.

📌 **Tip:** Pack a "finals day kit" with essentials like a water bottle, snacks, pens, pencils, and a calculator (if needed). Being prepared helps you feel calmer and more confident on exam days.

Week 14: Finishing Strong – Final Exams Week

Actionable Tips

- **Stick to your plan.** Follow the finals prep schedule you've been working on. Focus on one subject at a time, giving your full attention to each.
- **Prioritize your toughest exams.** Allocate extra study time to your most challenging courses. Tackle these early in the week to relieve stress.
- **Use practice tests.** If available, take practice exams to familiarize yourself with the format and timing of your finals.
- **Stay hydrated and eat well.** Fuel your brain with nutritious meals and drink plenty of water. Avoid heavy or junk food that might make you sluggish.
- **Review actively, not passively.** Instead of re-reading notes, quiz yourself, solve problems, or summarize key points from memory.

Motivational Advice

"This is it—the final stretch! Remember, all your hard work this semester has prepared you for this moment. Believe in yourself and take it one exam at a time. You're capable of more than you know, and no matter the outcome, you've already accomplished so much. Finish strong—you've got this!"

Fun Challenges

- **Pack a "finals survival kit."** Include snacks, water, highlighters, pens, and anything else you need for exams. **Bonus:** Share this idea with a friend!
- **Create a "pump-up" playlist.** Fill it with your favorite upbeat songs to listen to before exams and boost your confidence.
- **Celebrate small wins.** After each exam, treat yourself to something small—a coffee, a walk, or a quick chat with a friend. Acknowledge each step you take toward the finish line.

Weekly Checklist

- Stick to your study schedule and focus on one subject at a time.
- Allocate extra time for your most challenging exams.
- Take practice exams or complete review exercises for each subject.
- Stay hydrated, eat balanced meals, and get at least 7-8 hours of sleep.
- Use active study techniques like quizzing or summarizing key concepts.
- Pack a finals survival kit to keep yourself prepared and motivated.
- Reward yourself after each exam to celebrate your progress.

📌 **Tip:** On exam day, take 5 minutes before your test to do deep breathing exercises. This can reduce anxiety and improve focus during your exam.

Week 15: Wrapping Up and Reflecting on Your Semester

Actionable Tips

- **Submit all remaining assignments.** Double-check that you've completed and submitted every paper, project, and any lingering tasks for your classes.
- **Check your grades.** Review your progress in each class and calculate your final grades based on completed work and remaining exams or assignments.
- **Return borrowed materials.** Take care of returning library books, rented textbooks, or borrowed lab equipment to avoid late fees.
- **Clean and organize.** Tidy up your dorm room, desk, and digital files. Decluttering helps you start the next semester fresh and focused.
- **Reflect on the semester.** Write down what went well, what you learned, and areas where you'd like to improve. Use this reflection to set goals for next semester.

Motivational Advice

"You did it! Finishing your first semester is a huge accomplishment, and you should be proud of yourself. Reflect on how much you've grown, celebrate your wins (big and small), and take what you've learned to make next semester even better. Remember, this is just the beginning of your amazing college journey!"

Fun Challenges

- **Write a thank-you note.** Send a quick email or write a note to a professor, TA, or classmate who made a positive impact on your semester.
- **Create a memory board.** Collect photos, ticket stubs, or other keepsakes from the semester and arrange them into a collage or scrapbook to remember your first semester.
- **Plan a mini celebration.** Treat yourself and your friends to a fun outing or meal to celebrate finishing your first semester of college!

Weekly Checklist

- Submit all final assignments and check for missing tasks.
- Review your grades and calculate your final scores.
- Return borrowed books, materials, and supplies.
- Clean and organize your dorm room, desk, and digital files.
- Reflect on the semester: What went well? What could improve?
- Write a thank-you note to someone who helped you this semester.
- Plan a fun celebration or outing to mark the end of the semester.

📌 **Tip:** Reach out to your professors or TAs to thank them for their support. A quick thank-you email can help build positive relationships for the future.

Week 16: Rest, Recharge, and Plan for the Future

Actionable Tips

- **Take time to relax.** After a busy semester, give yourself permission to rest. Sleep in, enjoy your favorite hobbies, and spend quality time with friends and family.
- **Reflect on your first semester.** Ask yourself: What were your biggest accomplishments? What challenges did you face? How did you grow? Write these down to capture your journey.
- **Set goals for next semester.** Think about what you want to achieve academically, socially, and personally. Use what you learned this semester to guide your plans.
- **Update your resume.** If you gained any new skills, leadership roles, or experiences, add them to your resume while they're fresh in your mind.
- **Reconnect with home.** Spend time with loved ones and catch up on what you missed while at college. Share your experiences and accomplishments with them.

Motivational Advice

"You've crossed the finish line! Celebrate how far you've come—your first semester was a huge milestone. Rest, recharge, and reflect on all the ways you've grown. As you look ahead to next semester, know that you're capable of even more amazing things. The best is yet to come!"

Fun Challenges

- **Create a gratitude list.** Write down five things you're grateful for from this semester. Reflecting on positive experiences can boost your mood and motivation.
- **Have a "me" day.** Treat yourself to a full day of activities that make you happy—whether it's watching movies, cooking a favorite meal, or going on a solo adventure.
- **Plan a mini adventure with friends.** Go on a day trip, explore a new place, or just hang out with your college friends before heading home for the break.

Weekly Checklist

Take time to rest and recharge—no guilt allowed!

- Reflect on your accomplishments, challenges, and growth this semester.
- Set academic, personal, and social goals for next semester.
- Update your resume with new skills or experiences.
- Spend time with loved ones and share your semester highlights.
- Write a gratitude list to celebrate the positive moments of your first semester.
- Plan a fun outing or adventure with friends before the break ends.
- Update your "bucket List" in the front of the book.

📌 **Tip:** Start brainstorming a bucket list of things you want to do next semester, like joining a new club, visiting a specific spot on campus, or taking a fun elective.

```
T W O A L T W H A F T D G M D
C B X Q M A S U Z K Y O E W D
H Q Y H I R U D R X N R T J E
L F O E S O T N A I K M L C X
W R V A M O E D D O D F O A T
K E E L A M X H T R Y I S F R
O S R L T M T X V C Y R T E A
E H S N C A B L D P P E P T C
C M L I H T O S A A N A F E R
W A E G V E O T R R G L E R E
V N E H W F K V N T G A V I D
W 1 P T E B S P A Y M R X A I
C 5 A E J O U D P S U M K C T
X Y G R H I Q L Y M B R O K E
B S N O O D L E S F V R Q M G
```

Find These Words:
OVERSLEEP
NAP
NOODLES
LAUNDRY
MISMATCH
ALLNIGHTER
TEXTBOOKS
BROKE
DORMFIREALARM
ROOMMATE
CAFETERIA
FRESHMAN15
GETLOST
PARTY
EXTRACREDIT

Second Semester

Introduction: Semester Two – A Fresh Start for Bigger Goals

Congratulations on completing your first semester of college! You've already accomplished so much—from adjusting to a new environment to building routines, making connections, and tackling your first round of exams. Now, with semester one behind you, it's time to level up and make the most of everything you've learned so far.

The second semester is your chance to refine your habits, explore new opportunities, and set the stage for long-term success. Whether you want to boost your grades, make more friends, or start thinking about your career, this semester is full of fresh opportunities to grow.

What's Different About Semester Two?

You're no longer the "new kid." You've navigated the campus, figured out how to manage your schedule, and discovered what works for you (and what doesn't). Now it's time to build on that foundation:

- You can be more confident in your decisions and routines because you know what to expect.
- You have the freedom to push yourself further—whether that's joining new clubs, pursuing leadership roles, or exploring internships.
- You're more aware of your strengths and challenges, which helps you set smarter goals and plan effectively.

What's This Semester About?

This semester is all about growth and preparation for the future. It's about taking everything you learned in semester one and using it to go beyond just "surviving" college. This is your chance to:

- Sharpen your academic skills and aim for higher achievements.
- Strengthen your relationships with professors, classmates, and friends.
- Explore opportunities like internships, leadership roles, and career planning.
- Maintain balance and take better care of yourself as you pursue your goals.

How to Use This Guide

Just like last semester, this guide provides weekly tips, motivation, and challenges to help you thrive academically, socially, and personally. Each week will focus on a theme that builds on your successes from semester one:

- **Actionable Tips:** Easy, practical steps to keep you on track.
- **Motivational Advice:** Encouraging words to keep you inspired, even during stressful times.
- **Fun Challenges:** Small activities to make each week exciting and enjoyable.

You'll also find advice tailored to new opportunities and challenges unique to the second semester, like planning for summer internships, building long-term goals, and preparing for leadership roles.

Reflect and Recharge

Before diving into the semester, take some time to reflect on last semester:

- What are you proud of? Celebrate your wins, no matter how small.
- What challenges did you face? Think about how you can improve in those areas.
- What excites you about this semester? Write down your goals and dreams for the next few months.

Remember, the key to success is consistency. You've already proven you can handle the transition to college—now it's time to keep growing and thriving.

Get Ready to Thrive!

The second semester is a new chapter, full of opportunities to refine your skills, deepen your connections, and take bold steps toward your future. Whether it's acing your classes, building lasting friendships, or discovering your passions, this semester is yours to shape. You've got the tools, the confidence, and the determination to make it amazing. Let's dive in and make this semester your best one yet!

Week 1: Starting Fresh and Setting Goals

Actionable Tips

- **Review your syllabus.** Gather the syllabi for all your new classes, and highlight important dates like exams, project deadlines, and papers.
- **Set semester goals.** Write down 1-3 academic, personal, and social goals for the semester. Make them specific and realistic.
- **Create a new schedule.** Adjust your routine to match your new class times and commitments. Block out study time, meals, exercise, and downtime.
- **Organize your space.** Clean and declutter your dorm or workspace to create an environment that promotes focus and motivation.
- **Reconnect with friends.** Catch up with friends or classmates you haven't seen over the break. Rekindle connections to start the semester on a positive note.

Motivational Advice

"Semester two is your fresh start—a blank slate to redefine your routines, tackle new goals, and embrace every opportunity that comes your way. You've already proven you can handle college life, so take this chance to aim even higher. Remember, every small step you take today lays the foundation for a stronger, more confident you!"

Fun Challenges

- **Create a vision board.** Use pictures, quotes, and goals to make a visual representation of what you want to achieve this semester. Hang it somewhere you'll see it daily.
- **Plan a welcome-back hangout.** Organize a casual meetup with friends to swap stories about your break and share your goals for the semester.
- **Try something new.** Join a new club, sign up for a fitness class, or explore a new campus hangout spot to kick off the semester with excitement.

Weekly Checklist

- Review all syllabi and highlight important dates like exams and deadlines.
- Write down 1-3 academic, personal, and social goals for the semester.
- Create or adjust your schedule to fit your new classes and commitments.
- Clean and organize your dorm or workspace for a fresh start.
- Catch up with at least one friend or classmate after the break.
- Create a vision board or list of your semester goals and keep it visible.
- Explore a new club, activity, or spot on campus to try something new.

📌 **Tip:** Treat this semester as a fresh start! Write down three specific goals (academic, social, or personal) to focus on and track throughout the semester.

Week 2: Building Momentum and Staying Organized

Actionable Tips

- **Set up a task management system.** Use a planner, calendar app, or to-do list to organize your week. Include classes, assignments, study blocks, and personal activities.
- **Start early on assignments.** Don't wait until the last minute—set small daily goals for papers, projects, or readings to stay ahead of deadlines.
- **Review your goals.** Reflect on the goals you set last week. Are they realistic? Break them into smaller, actionable steps to make progress each week.
- **Create study routines.** Dedicate specific times each day for focused study sessions to develop consistent habits.
- **Introduce yourself in class.** Sit next to someone new or say hi to a professor during office hours to build connections early in the semester.

Motivational Advice

"The second week is where you set the tone for the rest of the semester. It's all about building momentum! A little extra effort now will save you time and stress later. Remember, consistency is key—each small step adds up to big wins."

Fun Challenges

- **Organize your digital space.** Clean up your laptop or phone by deleting old files, organizing folders, and backing up important documents.
- **Try a productivity hack.** Experiment with techniques like the Pomodoro method, time blocking, or habit stacking to boost your efficiency.
- **Explore campus resources.** Visit a part of campus you haven't checked out yet, like the career center, gym, or a quiet study spot.

Weekly Checklist

- Use a planner or app to map out your week, including classes, assignments, and study sessions.
- Start working on assignments or readings due later this month to stay ahead.
- Break down your goals into smaller, actionable steps to make weekly progress.
- Dedicate at least one hour each day to focused, distraction-free study.
- Introduce yourself to at least one new classmate or reconnect with a professor.
- Clean up your digital files and back up important documents.
- Explore a new campus resource or space to expand your comfort zone.

📌 **Tip:** Review last semester's mistakes and adjust your study habits. If you struggled with time management, create a weekly schedule now to stay ahead.

Week 3: Strengthening Connections and Finding Your Rhythm

Actionable Tips

- **Connect with classmates.** Introduce yourself to a few peers in each class. Exchange contact info for study groups or help with assignments.
- **Attend office hours.** Drop by your professor's or TA's office hours, even if it's just to ask a simple question. Building rapport early can be helpful later.
- **Fine-tune your routines.** Assess your current schedule and adjust where needed. Are your study times effective? Do you have enough downtime?
- **Engage in class.** Aim to participate at least once this week by asking a question, contributing to a discussion, or answering a professor's prompt.
- **Check your progress.** Review your progress toward your semester goals and tweak your plans if needed to stay on track.

Motivational Advice

"By now, you're starting to find your rhythm. This week is about taking those early connections and habits to the next level. Remember, the effort you put into relationships and routines now will make the rest of the semester smoother and more fulfilling. You're building a strong foundation for success!"

Fun Challenges

- **Try a campus event.** Look for a lecture, workshop, or club meeting happening this week and attend. It's a great way to expand your network and learn something new.
- **Plan a study meet-up.** Invite a friend or classmate to study together, even if you're working on different subjects. A little company can make studying more enjoyable.
- **Explore a new hobby.** Dedicate some time this week to trying a creative activity like painting, journaling, or learning a new skill—it's a great stress reliever.

Weekly Checklist

- Introduce yourself to at least two classmates and exchange contact information.
- Attend one professor or TA office hour to ask a question or discuss class material.
- Review your weekly schedule and adjust it for better balance, if needed.
- Participate in class by asking a question or sharing an idea in at least one session.
- Check your progress toward semester goals and make any necessary tweaks.
- Attend a campus event, lecture, or workshop to connect with new people or learn something new.
- Try a creative hobby or activity that helps you relax and recharge.

📌 **Tip:** Build relationships with professors by visiting office hours—this can help with career advice, internships, and even recommendation letters later on.

Week 4: Staying Balanced and Boosting Productivity

Actionable Tips

- **Prioritize self-care.** Block out time in your schedule for activities that recharge you, like exercise, meditation, or relaxing with a book.
- **Focus on one task at a time.** Use time-blocking or the Pomodoro method to stay focused and avoid multitasking, which can reduce productivity.
- **Review your workload.** Look at upcoming deadlines and plan your week to tackle assignments and projects in manageable chunks.
- **Cut back on distractions.** Identify your biggest time-wasters (e.g., social media, procrastination) and set limits using apps or timers.
- **Reach out for help.** If you're struggling with a subject or task, use campus resources like tutoring services or talk to your professors or peers for guidance.

Motivational Advice

"Balance is the key to productivity and happiness. You're not a machine—you're a human with needs for rest, fun, and connection. By managing your time wisely and making space for yourself, you'll achieve more and feel better doing it. Remember, it's not about doing it all—it's about doing what matters most."

Fun Challenges

- **Create a "power playlist."** Build a playlist of songs that motivate you and use it during study sessions or workouts.
- **Unplug for an hour.** Dedicate one hour to being completely offline—no phones, no screens, just time to reconnect with yourself or enjoy an offline activity.
- **Explore a new workout or activity.** Try yoga, a dance class, or even a quick jog around campus to get your energy flowing and reduce stress.

Weekly Checklist

- Dedicate time in your schedule for self-care activities like exercise, meditation, or hobbies.
- Use the Pomodoro method or time-blocking to focus on one task at a time.
- Review upcoming deadlines and break tasks into smaller, manageable steps.
- Identify and limit distractions by using focus apps or setting boundaries for social media.
- Reach out to campus resources, professors, or peers if you need help with academics.
- Create a "power playlist" to keep you motivated during study sessions or workouts.
- Unplug for at least one hour and enjoy an offline activity.

📌 **Tip:** Find a **study method that works for you**—some students need quiet libraries, others need background noise. Experiment and stick to what helps you focus best.

Week 5: Deepening Focus and Building Confidence
Actionable Tips

- **Refine your study habits.** Identify the study methods that have worked best for you so far and double down on them. Experiment with flashcards, group studies, or active recall if you're still figuring out what works.
- **Break down big tasks.** For upcoming projects or exams, divide the workload into smaller steps and tackle one at a time. This prevents overwhelm and boosts productivity.
- **Participate more in class.** Challenge yourself to ask a question or share an idea in each class this week. Active participation not only helps you learn but also builds confidence.
- **Review your goals.** Take a few minutes to check your progress toward your semester goals. Adjust any that feel unrealistic or revise your plans to stay on track.
- **Seek feedback.** Ask professors or peers for input on your assignments or performance. Constructive feedback can help you improve and build stronger connections.

Motivational Advice

"Week 5 is where the magic happens! By now, you've gained momentum, and this is your chance to level up. Remember, growth happens when you challenge yourself, take risks, and step outside your comfort zone. Confidence is built one small victory at a time—you're doing amazing!"

Fun Challenges

- **Start a "win journal."** Each day this week, write down one thing you accomplished, no matter how small. By the end of the week, you'll see how far you've come!
- **Host a study challenge.** Invite friends or classmates to a focused study session with fun rewards for meeting goals (like coffee or snacks).
- **Try a random act of kindness.** Compliment a classmate, help someone out, or leave an encouraging note. It's a great way to spread positivity and brighten your week.

Weekly Checklist

- Experiment with a new study habit or refine one that works for you (e.g., active recall, group studies).
- Break down a big project or assignment into smaller tasks and complete at least one step each day.
- Participate in class by asking a question, answering a prompt, or sharing an idea.
- Review your semester goals and adjust them as needed.
- Seek feedback from a professor or peer on an assignment or project.
- Start a "win journal" to track daily accomplishments, big or small.
- Perform one random act of kindness, like helping a classmate or leaving a positive note for someone.

📌 **Tip:** Challenge yourself academically—participate in class discussions, ask questions, and push yourself to think critically. Confidence grows with practice!

Week 6: Midterm Prep and Staying Calm

Actionable Tips

- **Create a midterm study plan.** List all your exams and deadlines, and prioritize the most challenging subjects. Break down study material into manageable chunks for each day.
- **Use active recall.** Instead of passively rereading notes, quiz yourself, practice problems, or explain concepts aloud to reinforce your understanding.
- **Attend review sessions.** Check if your professors or TAs are offering review sessions, and make time to attend. Use the opportunity to ask questions and clarify difficult topics.
- **Take care of your body.** Maintain regular meals, stay hydrated, and aim for 7–8 hours of sleep each night. Your brain works best when your body is well-rested and nourished.
- **Limit distractions.** Set up a quiet, clutter-free study environment and use focus apps to stay on task. Consider turning off notifications or putting your phone on airplane mode.

Motivational Advice

"Midterms are a chance to showcase all you've learned so far. Preparation is your secret weapon, and small, consistent steps will take you far. Remember, it's not about perfection—it's about doing your best with what you've got. Stay calm, trust yourself, and know that you're capable of great things!"

Fun Challenges

- **Create a study playlist.** Build a playlist of calm or upbeat tunes that help you focus during study sessions. Share it with friends for extra fun.
- **Reward yourself after each session.** Treat yourself to something small, like a snack, a short break, or a quick walk, every time you complete a study goal.
- **Write yourself a pep talk.** Jot down a motivational note or affirmation to read before exams. Remind yourself of your hard work and capability—it'll boost your confidence!

Weekly Checklist

- Create a study plan that outlines what to review each day for each subject.
- Prioritize your most challenging subjects and dedicate extra study time to them.
- Use active recall techniques like quizzing yourself, solving problems, or teaching concepts aloud.
- Attend at least one review session or visit your professor/TA during office hours for clarification.
- Stick to a consistent sleep schedule and get 7–8 hours of rest each night.

- Eat balanced meals, stay hydrated, and include brain-boosting snacks like nuts, fruit, or yogurt.
- Set up a distraction-free study environment and use tools like focus apps or timers.
- Reward yourself with small breaks or treats after completing study sessions or milestones.

📌 **Tip:** Start reviewing now! Make a list of what will be on each midterm and set aside small daily study sessions to avoid last-minute cramming.

Week 7: Recharging and Staying Consistent

Actionable Tips

- **Take a breather.** After midterms, give yourself permission to rest and recharge. Take a day (or at least a few hours) to do something that relaxes and refreshes you.
- **Review your progress.** Reflect on how you did during midterms. Celebrate your wins and identify areas for improvement without being too hard on yourself.
- **Reorganize your study materials.** Sort through notes, handouts, and digital files to declutter and make things easier to find for the rest of the semester.
- **Check in on your goals.** Are you still on track with your academic and personal goals? Make adjustments or set new ones if needed.
- **Focus on consistency.** Build a steady routine by dedicating daily blocks of time to studying, self-care, and downtime.

Motivational Advice

"You've made it through one of the toughest parts of the semester—now it's time to reset and keep moving forward. Rest is not a weakness; it's fuel for your growth. Use this week to rebuild your energy and strengthen your focus. Every step you take now is progress toward your bigger goals!"

Fun Challenges

- **Plan a self-care night.** Treat yourself to a relaxing evening with your favorite movie, a warm bath, or a creative hobby. Make it all about you!
- **Organize a mini adventure.** Explore a part of your campus or town you haven't visited yet, whether it's a park, café, or hidden study spot.
- **Do something kind for yourself.** Write yourself a positive note, treat yourself to a small gift, or plan something fun to look forward to this weekend.

Weekly Checklist

- Take at least one day (or a few hours) to rest and recharge after midterms.
- Reflect on your midterm performance and identify areas for improvement.
- Celebrate your wins from midterms, no matter how big or small.
- Reorganize your study materials, notes, and digital files to stay organized for the rest of the semester.
- Check your progress toward semester goals and adjust your plans if needed.
- Dedicate daily blocks of time for consistent study, self-care, and relaxation.
- Plan a self-care night with activities that help you unwind and relax.
- Do something kind for yourself, like writing a positive note or treating yourself to something you enjoy.

📌 **Tip:** Mid-semester fatigue is real! Schedule in self-care, whether it's a movie night, workout session, or simply a full night of sleep to recharge.

Week 8: Reflecting and Planning Ahead

Actionable Tips

- **Take stock of the semester so far.** Reflect on what's been working and what hasn't. Write down your biggest accomplishments and areas where you'd like to improve.
- **Revisit your goals.** Review the goals you set earlier this semester. Are you on track? If not, adjust them or create a plan to refocus.
- **Plan for upcoming deadlines.** Look ahead at projects, papers, and exams for the rest of the semester. Start breaking them into smaller tasks and set deadlines for each.
- **Check-in on your health.** Evaluate your sleep, nutrition, and exercise habits. Make adjustments to prioritize your well-being for the second half of the semester.
- **Network with professors or advisors.** Reach out to a professor, TA, or academic advisor to ask questions, share ideas, or get advice about your academic journey.

Motivational Advice

"Reaching the halfway point of the semester is a huge accomplishment! Now's the perfect time to reflect on how far you've come and prepare for what's ahead. Remember, progress isn't about perfection—it's about showing up and giving your best effort each day. You're building a foundation for success, one step at a time."

Fun Challenges

- **Create a gratitude list.** Write down five things you're grateful for from this semester. Reflecting on the positives can boost your mood and motivation.
- **Plan a fun weekend outing.** Treat yourself to a fun activity with friends, whether it's exploring a nearby town, having a picnic, or going to a campus event.
- **Start a new habit.** Choose one small, positive habit—like journaling, meditating, or stretching in the morning—and commit to it for the next week.

Weekly Checklist

- Reflect on your semester so far by listing accomplishments and areas for improvement.
- Revisit your semester goals and adjust them as needed for the second half of the term.
- Look ahead at upcoming assignments, projects, and exams, and create a plan to tackle them early.
- Evaluate your health habits (sleep, nutrition, exercise) and make any necessary adjustments.
- Visit or schedule time with a professor, TA, or academic advisor to discuss progress or ask questions.

- Create a gratitude list with five things you're thankful for this semester.
- Plan a fun weekend outing to recharge with friends or explore something new.
- Start a new habit, like journaling, meditating, or reading for personal growth.

📌 **Tip:** Check your grades so far—are you where you want to be? If not, reach out to professors for extra help or tutoring before finals season starts.

Week 9: Exploring Opportunities and Expanding Your Network

Actionable Tips

- **Visit your career center.** Schedule an appointment to explore internships, summer job opportunities, or career workshops. Take advantage of the resources available to you.
- **Start networking.** Connect with professors, advisors, and upperclassmen in your field of interest. Ask about their experiences and any advice they might have.
- **Polish your resume.** Update your resume with any new experiences or skills you've gained this semester. If you don't have one, start creating one using a template or career center guidance.
- **Research summer plans.** Begin looking into internships, research opportunities, or summer classes. Create a list of deadlines and application requirements to stay organized.
- **Attend a career-related event.** Check out any networking events, career fairs, or industry panels happening on campus this week.

Motivational Advice

"Your college years are the perfect time to explore your passions and take small steps toward your future career. Remember, you don't have to have it all figured out right now. Every connection you make and every opportunity you explore is a building block toward your goals. Be bold, take chances, and watch the possibilities unfold!"

Fun Challenges

- **Create a LinkedIn profile.** If you don't already have one, set up a profile and connect with classmates, professors, and others in your field of interest.
- **Shadow someone in your field.** Reach out to a professor or professional and ask if you can spend an hour learning about what they do—it's a great way to gain insights.
- **Plan a "dream job" brainstorm session.** Write down your ideal job, the skills needed for it, and the steps you can take in college to get there. Let yourself dream big!

Weekly Checklist

- Visit your career center to explore internships, job opportunities, or career resources.
- Connect with at least one professor, advisor, or upperclassman to discuss career or academic interests.
- Update your resume with new skills, experiences, or activities from this semester.
- Research summer opportunities, such as internships, classes, or volunteer programs, and note important deadlines.
- Attend a career-related event, like a career fair, networking session, or panel discussion.

- Set up or update your LinkedIn profile and connect with classmates, professors, and mentors.
- Shadow or have an informational interview with someone in your field of interest, if possible.
- Spend time brainstorming your "dream job" or career path, and list steps you can take to pursue it.

📌 **Tip:** Start looking for summer internships or jobs now! Many applications are due early—visit your career center for resume help and networking tips.

Week 10: Staying Motivated and Managing Mid-Semester Stress

Actionable Tips

- **Reorganize your priorities.** Review your schedule and assignments to identify your top priorities. Focus on completing the most important tasks first to reduce overwhelm.
- **Break down big tasks.** For projects, papers, or exams, divide the work into smaller, manageable chunks and tackle one step at a time.
- **Stick to your routines.** Keep up with your daily habits, like attending classes, dedicating time to study, and practicing self-care. Routines provide stability during busy weeks.
- **Ask for help.** If you're feeling stressed or stuck, reach out to professors, advisors, or friends. Don't hesitate to use campus resources like tutoring centers or counseling services.
- **Celebrate small wins.** Acknowledge and reward yourself for completing even small tasks, like finishing a paper draft or studying for an hour.

Motivational Advice

"Mid-semester can feel like a marathon, but you're stronger and more capable than you realize. Remember, it's okay to take things one step at a time. Progress is progress, no matter how small. Give yourself credit for how far you've come and stay focused on your goals—you've got this!"

Fun Challenges

- **Plan a "stress-busting" activity.** Dedicate time this week to something that helps you unwind, like playing a sport, doing yoga, or watching your favorite movie.
- **Switch up your study spot.** Find a new, inspiring place to study, whether it's a park, a cozy café, or a different part of the library. A change of scenery can boost focus.
- **Have a gratitude challenge.** Write down three things you're grateful for each day this week. Reflecting on the positives can improve your mood and motivation.

Weekly Checklist

- Reassess your priorities for the week and identify your top three most important tasks.
- Break down larger projects or assignments into smaller, manageable steps and set deadlines for each.
- Stick to your daily routines, including attending classes, studying, and practicing self-care.
- Reach out for help if needed by scheduling time with a professor, TA, or campus resource.
- Dedicate at least one hour to a stress-relief activity, like exercise, meditation, or creative hobbies.

- Write down three things you're grateful for each day to maintain a positive mindset.
- Set small rewards for completing tasks, like treating yourself to a favorite snack or short break.
- Plan an end-of-week activity with friends or family to relax and recharge.

📌 Tip: When motivation dips, change up your routine! Try a new study spot, join a new club, or set a small reward system to stay on track.

Week 11: Gearing Up for Finals and Staying Focused

Actionable Tips

- **Start preparing for finals early.** Review your syllabi and create a study schedule that includes time for each subject. Focus on the areas you find most challenging.
- **Organize your materials.** Gather your notes, past assignments, and study guides. Use folders or digital tools to keep everything accessible and organized.
- **Use active recall.** Practice quizzing yourself, solving problems, or teaching concepts to reinforce your understanding.
- **Attend review sessions.** Check if your professors or TAs are holding review sessions and prioritize attending them to clarify key concepts.
- **Stay consistent.** Dedicate time each day to studying, even if it's just for short intervals. Consistency will reduce last-minute cramming.

Motivational Advice

"Finals may seem daunting, but starting early and staying consistent will make all the difference. Remember, you've been building knowledge and skills all semester—this is your chance to show what you've learned. Believe in yourself, stay focused, and take it one step at a time. You've got this!"

Fun Challenges

- **Create a finals countdown.** Mark off days on a calendar and celebrate small victories as you complete your study goals.
- **Make studying fun.** Organize a themed study session with friends (e.g., "snack and study," "coffee and concepts") to mix productivity with enjoyment.
- **Plan a post-finals reward.** Think about how you'll celebrate after finals, like a day trip, special meal, or relaxing self-care day.

Weekly Checklist

- Review your syllabi and create a finals study schedule.
- Organize your notes and study materials for each class.
- Use active recall techniques to quiz yourself or solve problems.
- Attend at least one review session or office hour for additional help.
- Dedicate at least one hour per day to focused studying.
- Plan and schedule breaks to prevent burnout while studying.

- Start a finals countdown to track your progress and stay motivated.
- Organize a fun study session with friends or classmates.
- Decide on a post-finals reward to look forward to when exams are done.

📌 **Tip:** Make a finals countdown calendar! List each exam date and schedule review sessions now to avoid last-minute stress.

Week 12: Wrapping Up Projects and Building Momentum for Finals

Actionable Tips

- **Complete final projects and papers.** Focus on wrapping up major assignments this week. Break them into smaller tasks and set deadlines for each.
- **Start reviewing for finals.** Begin revisiting your study schedule and reviewing the most challenging material for each class. Early preparation will ease stress later.
- **Organize group projects.** If you're working on group assignments, set a meeting to finalize tasks and ensure everyone is on the same page.
- **Check deadlines twice.** Review all deadlines for assignments, papers, and exams to ensure nothing is missed.
- **Stay consistent with self-care.** Maintain healthy habits like regular meals, hydration, exercise, and sleep to keep your mind and body in top shape.

Motivational Advice

"You're in the home stretch—just a few weeks left! Now is the time to channel all the effort you've put in this semester and finish strong. Remember, every bit of work you do now will make finals week easier. Stay focused, keep pushing, and don't forget to take care of yourself along the way. You're almost there!"

Fun Challenges

- **Have a "work hard, play hard" day.** Dedicate the morning to focused work on assignments, and reward yourself in the evening with something fun, like a movie or game night.
- **Plan a mini celebration.** Treat yourself and friends to a quick outing (like coffee or ice cream) to celebrate completing a big project or paper.
- **Create a motivational study corner.** Decorate your desk or workspace with inspiring quotes, photos, or fun stationery to make studying feel more enjoyable.

Weekly Checklist

- Finish or make significant progress on final projects or papers.
- Start reviewing notes and study guides for finals, focusing on the hardest material first.
- Meet with group members to finalize any collaborative assignments.
- Double-check deadlines for all remaining assignments and exams.
- Maintain healthy habits: eat balanced meals, stay hydrated, and get 7-8 hours of sleep.
- Plan at least one "fun break" to recharge during the week.
- Decorate or organize your study space to boost motivation.
- Treat yourself to a small celebration after completing a major task.

📌 **Tip:** Don't leave papers or projects until the last minute! Try working on them a little each day—future you will thank you.

Fun Challenges

- **Have a "work hard, play hard" day.** Dedicate the morning to focused work on assignments, and reward yourself in the evening with something fun, like a movie or game night.
- **Plan a mini celebration.** Treat yourself and friends to a quick outing (like coffee or ice cream) to celebrate completing a big project or paper.
- **Create a motivational study corner.** Decorate your desk or workspace with inspiring quotes, photos, or fun stationery to make studying feel more enjoyable.

Weekly Checklist

- Finish or make significant progress on final projects or papers.
- Start reviewing notes and study guides for finals, focusing on the hardest material first.
- Meet with group members to finalize any collaborative assignments.
- Double-check deadlines for all remaining assignments and exams.
- Maintain healthy habits: eat balanced meals, stay hydrated, and get 7-8 hours of sleep.
- Plan at least one "fun break" to recharge during the week.
- Decorate or organize your study space to boost motivation.
- Treat yourself to a small celebration after completing a major task.

📌 **Tip:** Don't leave papers or projects until the last minute! Try working on them a little each day—future you will thank you.

Week 13: Finals Prep and Staying Motivated

Actionable Tips

- **Create a detailed study schedule.** Block out specific times for each subject and prioritize the most challenging topics. Stick to this schedule to avoid last-minute cramming.
- **Use past materials.** Review past quizzes, tests, and assignments to focus on key concepts that are likely to appear on finals.
- **Take regular breaks.** Incorporate short breaks into your study sessions using techniques like the Pomodoro method to stay fresh and focused.
- **Reach out for clarification.** Email professors or attend office hours if you have questions about exam material. It's better to ask now than to struggle later.
- **Practice self-care.** Balance studying with activities like exercise, meditation, or spending time with friends to keep stress levels in check.

Motivational Advice

"Finals week may seem overwhelming, but remember, you've made it through an entire semester of learning and growth. All your hard work has prepared you for this moment. Stay calm, take it one step at a time, and believe in yourself. Progress, not perfection, is the goal. You've got this!"

Fun Challenges

- **Host a "study buddy" session.** Invite a friend or classmate to study together, even if you're working on different subjects. It's more fun and keeps you accountable.
- **Create a reward system.** For every hour of studying or each task you complete, treat yourself to something small like a snack, a favorite song, or a short walk.
- **Design a motivational mantra.** Write down an encouraging phrase like "I've got this" or "One step closer" and place it where you'll see it while studying.

Weekly Checklist

- Finalize a detailed study schedule and stick to it.
- Review past quizzes, tests, and assignments to identify key concepts.
- Use active recall techniques like self-quizzing or teaching concepts aloud.
- Take regular breaks during study sessions to avoid burnout.
- Reach out to professors or TAs for clarification on exam material.
- Dedicate time to self-care activities like exercise, relaxation, or hobbies.

- Host or join a study session with friends or classmates.
- Create a small reward system to keep yourself motivated.
- Write or display a motivational mantra to inspire you throughout the week.

📌 **Tip:** Teach the material to someone else (even if it's just your stuffed animal). Explaining concepts out loud helps boost retention and understanding.

Week 14: Finals Week – Stay Calm and Crush It

Actionable Tips

- **Stick to your study schedule.** Follow the plan you've made, but be flexible if you need to adjust priorities based on your progress.
- **Review key concepts.** Focus on summaries, flashcards, and practice problems. Concentrate on the material you're less confident about.
- **Prepare for exam day.** Pack a "finals day kit" with essentials like pens, pencils, calculators, water, and snacks. Lay out everything you need the night before.
- **Pace yourself.** Don't try to study everything at once. Space out your sessions and dedicate time to rest and recharge.
- **Get plenty of sleep.** Avoid all-nighters—rest is critical for memory and focus. Aim for at least 7–8 hours of sleep before exams.

Motivational Advice

"This is it—the final stretch! Trust in all the work you've put in this semester. You've prepared, you've grown, and you're ready to show what you've learned. Stay calm, take deep breaths, and focus on one exam at a time. No matter what, finishing this semester is an achievement worth celebrating!"

Fun Challenges

- **Create a post-finals reward.** Plan a celebration, big or small, like treating yourself to a favorite meal, a movie night, or a day trip with friends.
- **Write yourself a pep talk.** Jot down encouraging words to read before each exam, reminding yourself of your hard work and resilience.
- **Plan a stress-busting activity.** After an exam, take a walk, listen to music, or watch a short video to decompress and reset for the next challenge.

Weekly Checklist

- Follow your study schedule and focus on reviewing key concepts.
- Use active recall methods like quizzes or teaching the material to yourself.
- Pack a finals day kit with all the essentials, including snacks and water.
- Dedicate time to rest and relaxation between study sessions to stay fresh.
- Get at least 7–8 hours of sleep before each exam.
- Take breaks during exams and study periods to clear your mind.

- Take breaks during exams and study periods to clear your mind.
- Write or display a pep talk or mantra to boost your confidence.
- Plan a post-finals celebration to look forward to after the week is over.
- Stay hydrated and eat nutritious meals to fuel your brain and body.

📌 **Tip:** Eat a healthy meal before your exams! Skipping breakfast or loading up on energy drinks can hurt your focus—fuel your brain for success.

Week 15: Wrapping Up the Semester and Celebrating Success

Actionable Tips

- **Submit final assignments.** Double-check that all papers, projects, and exams are completed and submitted before deadlines.
- **Review your grades.** Log into your student portal to check grades and assess your performance. Use this information to reflect on your academic journey.
- **Organize your materials.** Clean up your notebooks, digital files, and any other class materials. Archive what you want to keep for future reference.
- **Declutter your living space.** Tidy up your dorm, apartment, or workspace to create a fresh and relaxing environment for the break.
- **Reflect on your semester.** Write down your biggest achievements, lessons learned, and areas you want to improve next semester.

Motivational Advice

"You've reached the finish line, and that's something to celebrate! This semester was full of growth, challenges, and accomplishments. Take pride in how far you've come, no matter the hurdles you faced. Use this time to reflect on your journey and recharge for what's next. You've done amazing—be proud of yourself!"

Fun Challenges

- **Host a semester wrap-up gathering.** Invite friends to a casual get-together to share your favorite moments and celebrate the end of the semester.
- **Create a "highlight reel."** Write down or make a collage of your favorite moments, achievements, or memories from this semester.
- **Treat yourself.** Plan a special day or outing to relax and reward yourself for all your hard work.

Weekly Checklist

- Submit all final assignments and confirm they're received.
- Check your grades and reflect on your academic performance.
- Organize and archive your class materials for future reference.
- Clean and declutter your dorm or workspace for a fresh start.
- Write down your biggest wins and lessons learned this semester.

- Host or attend a celebration with friends to mark the end of the semester.
- Create a "highlight reel" to remember your favorite memories.
- Plan a self-care or fun day to recharge after a busy semester.

📌 Tip: Reflect on what you learned—beyond just classes. What personal growth did you experience? What habits do you want to carry into next year?

Week 16: Rest, Recharge, and Plan Ahead

Actionable Tips

- **Celebrate your accomplishments.** Take time to acknowledge all that you've achieved this semester, no matter how big or small. Reflect on your progress and growth.
- **Recharge your energy.** Dedicate time to rest and relaxation. Sleep in, enjoy hobbies, and spend quality time with friends and family.
- **Set goals for the break.** Decide how you'll use your time off—whether it's working, relaxing, learning a new skill, or preparing for next semester.
- **Plan for the future.** If you're pursuing internships, summer jobs, or research opportunities, finalize applications and deadlines now.
- **Organize your life.** Clean out your backpack, sort through old notes, and tidy up your digital and physical spaces to start fresh next semester.

Motivational Advice

"You made it! Completing a semester of college is no small feat, and you should be incredibly proud of yourself. Now is your time to rest, recharge, and dream about what's next. Use this break to celebrate your wins, reconnect with what makes you happy, and set your sights on new goals. The best is yet to come!"

Fun Challenges

- **Create a vision board.** Use magazines, photos, or digital tools to design a vision board for next semester or your long-term goals.
- **Plan a bucket list for the break.** Write down fun activities, hobbies, or trips you want to try during your time off.
- **Try something new.** Use the break to learn a new skill, like cooking a new recipe, practicing yoga, or starting a creative project.

Weekly Checklist

- Celebrate your semester accomplishments, big and small.
- Dedicate time to rest and recharge with sleep, hobbies, and self-care.
- Set goals for how you'll use your break, whether it's working, learning, or relaxing.
- Finalize applications for internships, jobs, or research opportunities.
- Clean and organize your physical and digital spaces for a fresh start.
- Create a vision board or write down goals for next semester.
- Plan fun activities or a bucket list for your break.
- Try at least one new skill or activity during your downtime.

📌 **Tip:** Take a real break! You earned it. Whether you relax at home, travel, or start a new hobby, allow yourself time to unwind before next semester.

Conclusion: Your Journey Has Just Begun

Congratulations! You've made it through your first year of college and completed this guide. What a ride it's been! From stepping onto campus as a wide-eyed freshman to navigating midterms, finals, friendships, and everything in between, you've grown in ways you might not have even realized. This first year was your foundation, and now you're ready to build an incredible future.

Reflect on Your Growth

Take a moment to reflect on all that you've accomplished this year:

- You've learned to manage your time, juggle responsibilities, and take care of yourself.
- You've built connections, explored opportunities, and discovered more about who you are.
- You've tackled challenges head-on and come out stronger on the other side.

Each win, no matter how small, is worth celebrating. And every challenge you faced was an opportunity to learn and grow. Give yourself credit for showing up, for trying, and for thriving in this brand-new chapter of life.

Looking Ahead

Your freshman year was just the beginning of your college journey. As you move forward:

- Keep exploring. College is the perfect time to try new things, take risks, and step outside your comfort zone. Join a club, sign up for an elective, or volunteer for something you're curious about.
- Keep learning. Academics are important, but so are the life skills you're building. Embrace every opportunity to grow intellectually, socially, and personally.
- Keep dreaming. Whether you're setting goals for next semester or envisioning your future career, let your dreams guide your decisions. Don't be afraid to aim high—you're capable of achieving amazing things.

Your Story is Just Beginning

This year was a chapter in the story of your life, but it's far from the end. The skills, habits, and lessons you've gained will carry you through not only the rest of college but also the challenges and opportunities that lie beyond. Remember that college isn't just about earning a degree; it's about discovering who you are, building your future, and creating memories that will last a lifetime.

Words of Encouragement

- You don't have to have everything figured out right now. Life is a journey, not a race.
- Be kind to yourself. Progress isn't always linear, and setbacks are part of growth.
- Trust yourself. You're more capable, resilient, and brilliant than you know.

A Final Challenge

As you close this book, take a moment to write yourself a letter. Include your hopes, dreams, and goals for the coming year. Seal it away and open it at the end of your sophomore year to see how far you've come. Let this act of reflection and anticipation remind you of how much you can achieve.

Thank You for Letting Me Be a Part of Your Journey

It's been a joy to guide you through your freshman year. You're off to an incredible start, and I can't wait to see what you'll accomplish next. Remember, the best is yet to come—and it's all waiting for you.

Here's to you and all the amazing things ahead. Now go out there, chase your dreams, and make your mark on the world. You've got this!

With pride and excitement for your journey,

Your College Guide

```
P S T U D Y C L Y W J H K T Z
H N F R S K A E W N B B P E Y
J W L X T B M C V C G M D X N
M L H L U A P T N R A Y Y T Q
W J X F D C U U Z E F Z M B D
T S E A E K S R A I F D I O N
U G X M N P L E F S N O Z O B
T C A T T A A A Z M G R T K L
O Q M M J C F D P K S M Q I U
R F N Z E K E Z R T Z Q P A Q
L L I B R A R Y V I O L J D R
Z C V L G K O M H W T P U Y R
J P P R O F E S S O R X V I P
T M T Y D C C A F E T E R I A
I R Z W C L A S S R O O M P E
```

Find These Words:
LIBRARY
DORM
LECTURE
PROFESSOR
TEXTBOOK
CAMPUS
STUDENT
LAPTOP
CAFETERIA
EXAM
BACKPACK
CLASSROOM
STUDY
TUTOR
GYM

✨ FUN

FRIENDS

Freshman Memories

HAPPY

💡 Advice for Next Year's Freshmen

Now that you've made it through your freshman year, it's time to help the next class! What advice would you give to incoming freshmen? Fill in the blanks and share your best tips, tricks, and survival strategies!

📚 **The Best Study Tip I Learned:**

🕐 **Time Management Hack That Saved Me:**

🍕 **The Best Place to Eat on Campus:**

🏫 **The Best Hidden Gem on Campus (Study Spot, Lounge, etc.):**

💡 Advice for Next Year's Freshmen

💰 **Money-Saving Tip for College Life:**

🎉 **The Most Fun Thing I Did Freshman Year:**

📌 **One Thing I Wish I Knew Before Starting College:**

🛏️ **Dorm Life Tip Every Freshman Should Know:**

🎒 **The Biggest Freshman Year Mistake to Avoid:**

💬 **One Piece of Advice I'd Give to Any New Student:**

🎓 College Bingo!

(Can You Get a Full Row?)

Check off everything you've done during your freshman year! Try to get a BINGO (or go for a blackout and complete them all!).

B	I	N	G	O
Got lost on campus	Pulled an all-nighter	Joined a club or organization	Went to a campus event for free food	Made a new friend in class
Took a nap in the library	Attended a sports game	Ate dining hall food that was *questionable*	Changed my major (or thought about it!)	Sat in the wrong class by accident
Used a random excuse to skip class	Spent way too much on coffee	Found a secret study spot	Had a late-night food run	Wore pajamas to class
Stayed in on a Friday night	Crammed for a test last minute	Walked across campus in the rain without an umbrella	Had an awkward encounter with a professor	Got excited about free campus merch
Studied for hours but retained nothing	Missed an assignment deadline (oops!)	Pulled off a great group project at the last minute	Lost my student ID	Had a deep convo with a roommate at 2 AM

🏆 **BINGO Goals:**

🎉 **One Row:** Freshman Rookie
🎉🎉 **Two Rows:** Campus Explorer
🎉🎉🎉 **Three Rows:** College Pro
🎉🎉🎉🎉 **Four Rows:** Dorm Legend
🎉🎉🎉🎉🎉 **Full Card (Blackout!):** True College Icon

Freshman Year Superlatives

Best Study Spot: _____

Most Inspiring Professor: _____

Favorite Late-Night Snack: _____

Most Stressful Assignment: _____

Best Campus Event: _____

Most Likely to Skip Class for Coffee: _____

🏆 Dorm Room Awards

(Because Every Dorm Deserves an Award!)

Your dorm room was more than just a place to sleep—it was your study spot, hangout space, and home for the year. What kind of personality did your room (or your roommate's room) have? Fill out these Dorm Room Superlatives to award your space the recognition it deserves!

🎖️ Best Snack Stash: _____

🖼️ Most Creative Decorations: _____

🛏️ Comfiest Bed Setup: _____

🌱 Best Use of a Tiny Space: _____

🎮 Ultimate Entertainment Setup: _____

📚 Most Likely to Be a Study Zone: _____

🧼 Neatest & Most Organized Room: _____

🤯 Most "Organized Chaos" (A.K.A., Controlled Mess!):

_____

🔌 Most Likely to Have Every Charger & Tech Gadget:

_____

🌈 Best Room Aesthetic: _____

🎉 Most Popular Hangout Spot: _____

😂 Most Likely to Have a Random Item No One Else Has:
_____

🏆 Overall Dorm Room Award Title: "Most Likely To"
_____

📌 **Roommate Edition!**

👯 Best Late-Night Conversations With:
_____

📺 Most Likely to Binge-Watch Shows With:
_____

🍕 Most Likely to Order Late-Night Food With:
_____

😂 Funniest Roommate Moment:
_____

🎓 My College Favorites

(A Snapshot of My Freshman Year!)

College is full of unforgettable moments, new experiences, and discoveries about yourself. Use this page to record your favorite parts of your freshman year so you can look back and relive the memories!

📚 Favorite Class: _____

🏫 Favorite Campus Building or Spot: _____

👨‍🏫 Favorite Professor: _____

📖 Favorite Book I Read for Class (or Fun!): _____

🍕 Favorite Dining Hall Meal or Snack: _____

☕ Favorite Coffee Spot or Late-Night Hangout: _____

🎉 Favorite Campus Event:
_____

🎶 Favorite Song That Defined My Year:
_____

💡 Favorite Lesson I Learned This Year:
_____

👯 Favorite New Friend(s) I Met:
_____

🏆 Favorite Personal Achievement:
_____

💭 Favorite Memory from Freshman Year:
_____

⭐ One Thing I'll Miss About My Freshman Year:
_____

📌 One Thing I Can't Wait for Next Year:
_____
_____

Autographs

Photo Wall

www.ingramcontent.com/pod-product-compliance
Lightning Source LLC
Chambersburg PA
CBHW050649160426
43194CB00010B/1876